99 ½
Spooky Jokes, Riddles, & Nonsense

**Written and illustrated
by Holly Kowitt**

SCHOLASTIC INC.

New York Toronto London Auckland Sydney

ISBN 0-590-93776-6

12 11 10 9 8 7 6 5   8 9/9 0 1/0

Printed in the U.S.A.   40

First Scholastic printing, October 1996

To Jason,
who scares easily

MONSTER JOKES

Monster #1: Am I late for dinner?
Monster #2: Yes, everyone's eaten.

Why did the monster bring a root beer to Pittsburgh?

To have something to wash it down with!

What do monsters eat for dessert?

Baked Alaska.

Why did the monster eat the North Pole?

He was in the mood for a frozen dinner.

How do monsters like movie stars?

Medium rare.

Monster #1: Can you lend me an ear?
Monster #2: Yes, but I'll need it back.

MONSTER'S BOOKSHELF

Dare You to Touch It
  by Harry I. Ball

My Life as a Private Eye
  by Sy Klopps

Tales That Will Shock You
  by Frank N. Stein

What Happened to the Teacher?
  by I. A. Tim

TOO GHOUL FOR SCHOOL

Why did the witch stay home from school?
She had a wicked cold.

What do naughty ghosts use in school?
Cheat sheets.

Why can't the Invisible Man pass school?

Because the teacher always marks him absent.

What happens when you bring a witch to the school cafeteria?

Food fright!

What do vampires wear in the fall?

Their bat-to-school clothes.

Teacher: Why didn't you finish the book I assigned?
Monster: I'm not supposed to eat between meals!

WITCH'S MENU

Baked Beings

Corn on the Cobweb

Scrambled Legs

Jello Mould

Chicken Poodle Soup

Screamed Spinach

Bug Juice

GO TO YOUR BROOM!

What do you have when you cross a witch and a clown?

A brew-ha-ha.

Where do witches go to have their hair done?

Ugly parlors.

Did you hear about the witch no one was afraid of?

She was having a bad scare day.

Why do witches send greeting cards?

To show that they scare.

BE QUIET
AND COMB YOUR FACE

What does a werewolf say to the barber?

"Just take a little off the knuckles."

Where do werewolves go shopping?

The maul.

Why did the werewolf wear a sparkly gown and tiara?

She wanted to be a hairy princess.

How do you send a package to a werewolf?

By hairmail.

OBNOXIOUS KNOCK-KNOCKS

Knock-knock.
Who's there?
Gruesome.
Gruesome who?
Gruesome stinkweed, do you want any?

Knock-knock.
Who's there?
Ivan.
Ivan who?
Ivan to suck your blood.

Knock-knock.
Who's there?
Witch.
Witch who?
Witch one of you can fix my broomstick?

HOW'S WORK?

Creature from the Black Lagoon:
  "I'm swamped."

Abominable Snowman:
  "Not so hot."

Cyclops:
  "It's looking better."

Vampire:

"*Draining.*"

Invisible Man:

"*I'm hardly there.*"

Two-headed Monster:

"So-so."

Gravedigger:

"I'm really throwing myself into it."

LOATHSOME LETTERS

Why is the letter "T" ticklish?

Because it makes a witch twitch!

Why do you invite the letter "R" to a Halloween party?

Because it makes fiends friends.

Why is the letter "H" scary?

Because it makes an owl howl.

GOOD MOANING, EVERYONE!

Ghost #1: Should I visit my old house?
Ghost #2: Honey, if you've got it, haunt it!

What do ghosts do at camp?
Short-sheet each other's beds.

Why did the ghost go on safari?
He liked big-game haunting.

What's a ghost's favorite Mother Goose story?

Little Boo Peep.

What do baby ghosts wear?

Pillowcases.

What do you use to erase a ghost?

White-out.

HAVE YOU EVER SEEN...

a strawberry shake?

a pumpkin squash?

a lamb chop?

an ice (s)cream?

TOMB IT MAY CONCERN

What did one zombie say to another?

"Get a life!"

Did you hear about the comedian who created Frankenstein's Monster?

He had him in stitches.

What did the Invisible Man's mother say to him?

"We never see you anymore!"

What do the Swamp Thing and the Blob do when they get together?

Talk about old slimes.

Spook #1: How was the party at the cemetery last night?
Spook #2: Lousy. The place was dead.

Why does a mummy make a bad birthday gift?

He takes a long time to unwrap.

Did you hear the story about the zombie who keeps rabbits?

It's hare-raising.

Did you hear they had to close skeleton school?

They didn't have a student body.

HOW DID YOU FEEL
WHEN YOU SAW A GHOST?

Baby:

"Rattled!"

Fireman:

"Alarmed!"

Tennis Racket:

"Unstrung!"

Tree:

"Petrified!"

Electrician:

"*Shocked!*"

Frog:

"*Jumpy!*"

THINGS THAT GO BUMP IN THE NIGHT

Why are garbage trucks scary?

They go dump in the night.

Why are gas station attendants scary?

They go pump in the night.

Why are rabbits scary?

They go jump in the night.

FOOD FRIGHT

What do you serve a skeleton for dinner?

Spare ribs.

What do you give the Swamp Thing when he's thirsty?

A Slushie.

What kind of cheese does Frankenstein's Monster like?

Muenster.

What do you serve the Creature from the Black Lagoon for dessert?

Mud pies.

GOOD THINGS NOT TO DO WITH A MONSTER

Lend him an ear.

Give him a hand.

Spill your guts.

Keep an eye on him.

Offer him your heart.

EXCUSE ME, BUT
YOUR TEETH ARE IN MY NECK

What do you call twin vampires?

Blood brothers.

Why did the vampire take a vacation?

He was under too much blood pressure.

Is the vampire a close friend of yours?

Well, I wouldn't stick my neck out for him.

Why did the vampire go to the beauty parlor?

He was having a bat hair day.

Librarian: What kind of book do you want this time?
Dracula: Something in a similar vein.

What happened to the vampire who had his lunch stolen?

He lost a lot of blood.

Where do vampires put their money?

Blood banks.

How did you feel after seeing Dracula?

Drained.

What kind of jokes do vampires tell?

Neck-neck jokes.

COLD CUTS

Why did the Abominable Snowman bring a shovel on his first date?

He wanted to break the ice.

What did the Abominable Snowman give the vampire?

Frostbite.

What does the Abominable Snowman play at recess?

Freeze tag.

PLEASE, NO MORE MONSTER JOKES!

What kind of flowers does a monster give his girlfriend?

Stinkweed.

Why did the monster get sick after visiting the Empire State Building?

He bit off more than he could chew.

Monster #1: How was the restaurant?
Monster #2: The waiter was excellent!

What does a monster call a town of fifty people?

An appetizer.

MONSTER MENU:

Sloppy Joe

Big Mac

Reuben Sandwich

Apple Betty

Peppermint Patty

Mother Monster: What happened in school today?

Kid Monster: The teacher grilled me.

Monster #1: Nice car.

Monster #2: It better be. It cost an arm and a leg.

Why was the monster a bad dancer?

He had four left feet.

What does Godzilla drive?

A monster truck.

How does Godzilla get exercise?

On the Stairmonster.

How does Godzilla like his potatoes?

Monster-mashed.

TWO-HEADED MONSTERS:
HUBBA-HUBBA!

Favorite dessert:

Bon-bons.

Favorite dance:

Cha-cha.

Favorite instrument:

Tom-tom.

How do you call a two-headed monster?

"*Yo-yo!*"

Why do two-headed monsters make bad drivers?

Because they double park.

What do you call a two-headed monster who walks across a muddy street?

A dirty double-crosser.

YO, CYCLOPS!

Where can you see a Cyclops dance?

At an eyeball.

What happened when you realized you were a Cyclops?

It was a real eye-opener.

Where does a Cyclops go after fifth grade?

To junior eye school.

HALF-JOKE

How does a monster feel after _____?
Full.